Bedtime Wishes for a better world with Kai and Lani

WRITTEN BY
TIMNA SITES

ILLUSTRATED BY
NADIA RONQUILLO

As a mother, middle child with eight siblings, and a child welfare attorney, Timna knows the importance of a childhood filled with love, play, learning, and positive reinforcement in parenting. In this bedtime routine book, children will use their imaginations to learn values such as empathy, gratitude, respect, equality and courage. Learn more about the author at www.TimnaSites.com

Bed Time Wishes for a Better World with Kai and Lani
© 2024 by Timna Sites

Written by Timna
Illustrated by Nadia Ronquillo

All rights reserved. No part of this publication may be reproduced, stored in retrieval system, or transmitted in any form by any means electronic, mechanical, photocopy, or recording in any form — except for brief quotations in printed reviews without prior permission from the authors.

This is a work of fiction. Names, characters, places and incidents are products of the authors' imaginations or are used fictitiously and are not to be construed as real. Any resemblance to actual events, locales, organizations or persons living or dead, is entirely coincidental. While all attempts have been made to verify the information provided in this publication, neither the author nor the publisher assumes any responsibility for errors, omissions, or contrary interpretations of the subject matter herein. Interpretation and application are the sole responsibility of the purchaser or reader. The advice and strategies found within may not be suitable for every situation. This work is sold with the understanding that neither the author or the publisher are held responsible for the results accrued from the advice in this book. You should consult with a health professional for further details and further actions.

ISBN: 979-8-9905091-4-6

Mahalo nui loa to
Terry who showed me
Aloha by making me
part of her Ohana.

Kai and Lani love to play with bots, stuffies and goo.

They imagine they can fly
and save the whole world too!

get dressed and flush,

they jump in bed to read
of adventures and magic,
or bugs and gadgets,
and the love that we all need.

With songs and hugs, blankets all snug,

They're safe and sound
with Tabby and Hound
and no thoughts left for fright.

They say these words to end their day with gratitude most precious.

To think of more than just themselves, they say their bedtime wishes.

May we always treat others with care and respect and honor all those who have come and have left.

May we never forget what others went through to make this life better for me and for you.

And when we see something that's so very wrong, may we make it right, take courage, be strong,

so each life is brilliant, each future shines bright,
just like the centillions of stars in the night.

Now they take deep breaths, and stay real still,

close eyes tight, stay calm until...

they feel so heavy...

heavy...
heavy

and see they're in magical dreamlands already.

Printed in the USA
CPSIA information can be obtained
at www.ICGtesting.com
LVHW061038201124
796612LV00024B/91